Eat Like a Local

BOOK DESCRIPTION

Are you excited about planning your next trip? Do you want an edible experience? Would you like some culinary guidance from a local? If you answered yes to any of these questions, then this Eat Like a Local book is for you. *Eat Like a Local - North Carolina* by Sarah Gurganus offers the dish on food culture and culinary tradition in North Carolina. Culinary tourism is an import aspect of any travel experience. Food has the ability to tell you a story of a destination, its landscapes, and culture on a single plate. Most food guides tell you how to eat like a tourist. Although there is nothing wrong with that, as part of the Eat Like a Local series, this book will give you a food guide from someone who has lived at your next culinary destination.

In these pages, you will discover advice on having a unique edible experience. This book will not tell you exact addresses or hours but instead will give you excitement and knowledge of food and drinks from a local that you may not find in other travel food guides.

Eat like a local. Slow down, stay in one place, and get to know the food, people, and culture. By the time you finish this book, you will be eager and prepared to travel to your next culinary destination.

OUR STORY

Traveling has always been a passion of the creator of the Eat Like a Local book series. During Lisa's travels in Malta, instead of tasting what the city offered, she ate at a large fast-food chain. However, she realized that her traveling experience would have been more fulfilling if she had experienced the best of local cuisines. Most would agree that food is one of the most important aspects of a culture. Through her travels, Lisa learned how much locals had to share with tourists, especially about food. Lisa created the Eat Like a Local book series to help connect people with locals which she discovered is a topic that locals are very passionate about sharing. So please join me and: Eat, drink, and explore like a local.

TABLE OF CONTENTS

BOOK DESCRIPTION
OUR STORY
TABLE OF CONTENTS
DEDICATION
ABOUT THE AUTHOR
HOW TO USE THIS BOOK
FROM THE PUBLISHER
An Entire Section On Barbecue
1. Because We Take Barbecue Very Seriously
2. "Barbecue Historian" Is A Real Job Around These Parts
3. There's An Actual Barbecue Law
4. Barbecue Must Be Eaten With Specific Side Items
5. Krispy Kreme Donuts - No Really, You Are Welcome
6. Pepsi, The Original Colon Cleanse
7. Cheerwine (And Moonshine And NASCAR)
8. Texas Pete - Not Texan And A Little Racist
9. Bojangles' V. Hardee's (V. newcomer Cook Out)
10. Mount Olive Gets In A Pickle
11. Nabs, An Unproven Conspiracy Theory
Home Cooking We Take Credit For
12. Shrimp And Grits Was Invented Here
13. Fried Green Tomatoes Are A Delicacy

14. Forget Toast! We Do Biscuits And Gravy
15. Unless We're In The Mountains Where We Replace The Sausage With...Chocolate
16. We're At War With Virginia And Georgia About Who Invented Brunswick Stew
17. Pimento Cheese - The Best Ancestry Test For Native North Carolinians
18. Carolina Style Anything
19. Where Mashed Potatoes Become Dessert
20. Sandwich Bread Is A Lowly Replica Of A Biscuit
21. Boiled Peanuts, A Staple That Should Be Removed
22. Okra Isn't From Here But It Can Stay
23. Fried Collards, A Superfood - Kind Of
24. Living In Sin
25. Livermush (And Other Weird Meats)
26. Bill Friday's Peanut Brittle
27. The Most Humble Pie
28. The Most Unnative Native Food Of All Time
29. Sonker or Cobbler?

Fun Food Facts

30. Weird & Delicious Food Festivals
31. Fish Camps Are Better Than Michelin Stars
32. Oddly Specific State Foods
33. More Turkeys Than People

Eat Like a Local

34. Almost Half Of America's Sweet Potatoes Are Grown in Eastern NC
35. The Largest Pork Display Somewhere
36. We Make Wine And Fry A Lot Of Really Big Things
37. Really Old Wine

Where to Eat

38. Ashley's Dynasty
39. Hunters...But Vegan
40. Barbecue Joints
41. More Donuts
42. Seafood
43. Asheville
44. Chapel Hill
45. Charlotte
46. Durham
47. Greensboro & Winston-Salem
48. Raleigh
49. Wilmington
50. Two Bonus Restaurants In The Middle Of Nowhere But Too Good To Leave Out

Conclusion

Other Resources

READ OTHER BOOKS BY CZYK PUBLISHING

DEDICATION

This book is dedicated to Lilith Castellano. Thanks for being my eating-our-way-through-North-Carolina-and-Guatemala partner for the last twenty years.

ABOUT THE AUTHOR

Sarah Gurganus is a teacher, writer, and community organizer raised in Wilmington, North Carolina, though her family hails from Martin County on the east coast and Ashe County in the Appalachian Mountains. She is the director of the non-profit organization Fortaleza, Mujer!, dedicated to ending gender-based violence in Guatemala, where she spends the bulk of her non-North Carolina time. When she isn't working, she enjoys exploring wherever life has taken her for the day, and makes time for her family, good food, good books, and cats.

Sarah grew up in the farm kitchens of her grandmothers, sneaking produce directly from the field in her grandfathers' crops, in her mother's bakery, and eating fresh-caught seafood on docks and in sand. She's eaten her way through a few countries and continents, and nothing compares to what she was raised on in North Carolina.

Eat Like a Local

HOW TO USE THIS BOOK

The goal of this book is to help culinary travelers either dream or experience different edible experiences by providing opinions from a local. The author has made suggestions based on their own knowledge. Please do your own research before traveling to the area in case the suggested locations are unavailable.

Travel Advisories: As a first step in planning any trip abroad, check the Travel Advisories for your intended destination.
https://travel.state.gov/content/travel/en/traveladvisories/traveladvisories.html

North Carolina Climate

	High	Low
January	51	30
February	55	33
March	63	39
April	72	47
May	79	56
June	86	65
July	89	68
August	87	67
September	81	60
October	72	49
November	62	39
December	53	32

GreaterThanaTourist.com

Temperatures are in Fahrenheit degrees.
Source: U.S. climate data

FROM THE PUBLISHER

Traveling can be one of the most important parts of a person's life. The anticipation and memories that you have are some of the best. As a publisher of the *Eat Like a Local*, Greater Than a Tourist, as well as the popular *50 Things to Know* book series, we strive to help you learn about new places, spark your imagination, and inspire you. Wherever you are and whatever you do I wish you safe, fun, and inspiring travel.

Lisa Rusczyk Ed. D.
CZYK Publishing

Eat Like a Local

The secret of success in life is to eat what you like and let the food fight it out on the inside.

- Mark Twain

(who must have eaten

at least one meal in North Carolina)

North Carolina
United States

North Carolina, like the rest of the American South, can tell a delicious history about the food we put on our plates, but it's a dark one, too. Our food culture is a blend of Native American, African, English, and Moravian dishes, and the influence came to us in that order.

The first European migrants to North Carolina attribute their survival to the teachings of Native Americans, who survived on a corn-based diet, which explorer John Lawson called The Most Useful Grain in the World. The rest of their food was fairly versatile, as North Carolina has always been fertile farmland, and Native Americans here were both farmers and hunter-gatherers.

North Carolina's penchant for food as an opportunity for a social gathering is often given Native American roots, although it's seen in other cultures as well. Native Americans had very active lifestyles, so they had huge caloric needs. They'd only stop their work to eat, and often gathered at special events to gorge themselves on foods to such an extent that European settlers who witnessed it and were invited often couldn't keep up. This particular habit is attributed to their need for high intake, and is mirrored today in customs of modern North Carolinians, where farming culture means we gather for big meals together before and after work, and for many celebrations in which we gather with our entire families, social groups, or communities.

While there are defined roots in Native American dishes, the bulk of our culinary history is African. Why? It's pretty clear: the Southern United States, particularly states on the Eastern Seaboard like North Carolina, relied on slave labor, and put the finest cooks in their kitchens. Most of these slaves, or their parents, had come directly from Africa, so they brought the traditions they knew to plantation kitchens.

Those forced into work in other parts of plantations were given meager food rations of low quality and adapted their traditional dishes with the resources available. The foods they perfected in this manner made their way into the kitchens of their owners. These foods rich in spirit became richer still with finer ingredients available, and the adapted dishes became popular throughout the South. Dishes based in rice, okra, pork, and collard greens almost all are derived from African fare.

Though the original European migrants to North Carolina were mostly British, that particular food culture didn't survive through the years. They came here ill-equipped for survival in the environment and they themselves in many written histories attributed their success to Native Americans who fed them for a time, taught them how to cook, and showed them how to grow and hunt. The selection of options in the bountiful farmland here was really more plentiful than what they'd experienced in their homeland, and so the dishes that survived that time are well-preserved as being authentically British and are present currently more as international flavors reintroduced in our global culture now than having been passed down from original settlers.

Moravian history is a slightly different story. Especially in the west, there is a strong presence even today of the foods these German missionaries introduced. Coming to North Carolina by way of Pennsylvania in the mid-eighteenth century, the Moravian church founded most of the area that is today Forsyth County, where one of our largest cities, Winston-Salem, is located. Their culinary traditions, particularly sweets in a time of ration, took hold and haven't let go of North Carolina culture.

Modern Carolina cuisine, especially in urban areas, is now more heavily influenced by groups from all over the world, as we're blessed to have some of the most diverse migrant communities in the country. We have some of the best Mediterranean and especially Greek and Turkish restaurants to be found, and some of the best pizza south of New York and west of Italy, depending on the style you're looking for. Asian and African flair abounds. Whatever you're craving while you visit, if you're willing to hunt and want to take a brief break from the country kitchens of Carolina or the monotonous chain restaurants, you can find it here.

AN ENTIRE SECTION ON BARBECUE

Barbecue is the third rail of North Carolina politics. - John Shelton Reed, essayist, sociologist, truth-speaker

1. BECAUSE WE TAKE BARBECUE VERY SERIOUSLY

In North Carolina, families divide over the barbecue rift. In fact, while any other Southerner defines their geography by their residence below the Mason Dixon line, in our state the true continental divide splits the Old North State into east and west. The one thing the two factions agree on is that barbecue is only proper when it's pork - sure we'll eat barbecue chicken or beef, and we'll even enjoy it, but that's just another food entirely and practically exotic.

The important difference is more nuanced. Most Americans think of barbecue as a grill to slap meat on in the backyard, or maybe a tangy tomato sauce. But a proper native North Carolinian knows barbecue isn't a verb or an adjective, and it's not a backyard stovetop (we call those grills) or an event to which you invite the neighbors (we call them pig-pickins, no final "g" necessary). It's slow-cooked pork and nothing else. In the eastern part of the state, the whole hog is roasted, chopped, and mixed with vinegar and red pepper flakes. To the west of Raleigh, only the shoulder is used and the sauce has a tomato base more similar to the flavor commonly associated around the country with the word "barbecue."

2. "BARBECUE HISTORIAN" IS A REAL JOB AROUND THESE PARTS

That's because the debate had to be settled, and the verdict is in. Eastern-style barbecue is the OG, the original oldtimer based in the Native American and African, and even Spanish, culinary traditions that influence a great deal of the regional cuisine. The great barbecue battle began sometime around the onset of World War I, and it's a toss-up which one influenced the state more.

Ketchup was invented in 1876 and that was the decline that began the west's great betrayal. In the Piedmont region of the state, barbecue pitmasters began mixing the tomato paste into the vinegar sauce. At the same time, they began only using the shoulder of the pig. Now some western Carolinians would argue that the shoulder is the tastiest part, implying this makes the barbecue superior, but we coastal folks know the tomato base smothers the meat's flavor while the vinegar enhances it. We also know that the shoulder is the cheapest part of the hog and the

Eat Like a Local

hillbillies in the west aren't aristocrats like those of us in the flatlands.

3. THERE'S AN ACTUAL BARBECUE LAW

I know what you're thinking - there are crazy laws everywhere we can all chuckle about. Some states outlaw ice cream in your pocket and in Florida, your elephant may have a parking ticket on it when you get back from shopping if you didn't feed the parking meter. But those are old rules, you tell yourself. We're rational these days.

Not over barbecue, we aren't - not in North Carolina. Yes, from 2005 to 2007, we taxpayers paid our elected officials to debate barbecue in the State House. The debacle started innocently enough - some silly travel magazine no one has ever heard of, called Travel + Leisure, named the Lexington Barbecue Festival one of the Top Ten Food Festivals in the Country. (Lexington is recognized as the birthplace of the western style, which is also sometimes called Lexington-style. And fine, it's a fantastic festival.)

Some congresspeople from west of the dividing line got big heads and introduced bills in both the House and Senate naming the annual event the official state barbecue festival. The vote passed one chamber but barbecue purists in the other were having none of it.

There was no way we easterners would allow the Lexington heathens to own the claim to the official state barbecue festival. That is entirely too specific and might lead one to believe that the ketchup monstrosity was the preferred and approved take. It's simply not true and we were ready to pick up our muskets and fight. One esteemed journalist, Dennis Rogers of the Raleigh News & Observer, was absolutely robbed of the Pulitzer Prize that year after he declared, "[p]eople who would put ketchup in the sauce they feed to innocent children are capable of most anything."

After two long years of battle, cute little schoolchildren were the future and led the way when a fourth grade class wrote to their Davidson County representatives and suggested the annual shin-dig be named the official state food festival. Somehow to me that sounds even more definitive than just qualifying in the barbecue category and not every food there is, but at least it sparked discussion.

Eventually peace accords were signed in the form of House Bill 433, which dubbed the Lexington festival "the official food festival of the North Carolina Piedmont Triad." The rest of the state agreed to it, because we all know the Piedmont Triad has inferior food anyway, so it does nothing to sully the reputation of the East's sensory masterpieces.

No casualties were reported in the war.

4. BARBECUE MUST BE EATEN WITH SPECIFIC SIDE ITEMS

Barbecue must be eaten with slaw and hushpuppies. That's not a state law but we do hold it sacred. Whether the slaw is mayonnaise-based or has some tomato sauce mixed in depends upon which side of the border from you hail, and carrots and pickles are a matter of preference too. The hushpuppy debate may sometimes get as heated as the barbecue one, though most often if you find the hushpuppies to be made differently than your grandmother and all your aunts, you just eat them anyway and enjoy them marginally less.

There are more than a dozen other side items that can be paired with a plate of barbecue - collards or cabbage, deviled eggs, potato salad or boiled potatoes, sweet potatoes or stewed apples, macaroni and cheese, rutabagas, Brunswick stew, various bean preparations, and more. Some are so unique and important to North Carolina culture they merit their own sections here. We each have our favorites but blood is only shed over the barbecue itself.

Food Brands You Can Thank North Carolina For

You have to stay true to your heritage; that's what your brand is about - Alice Temperley, fashion designer

5. KRISPY KREME DONUTS – NO REALLY, YOU ARE WELCOME

If Krispy Kreme isn't evidence that North Carolina is the Promised Land, then nothing else is. But did you know these donuts are direct descendents of the famed beignets of New Orleans? In 1923, a man by the name of Vernon Rudolph purchased a top secret recipe for yeast donuts from a French chef in New Orleans.

He opened his first donut shop with an uncle in Paducah, Kentucky, but it was a difficult run at the height of the Great Depression. After trying a few more locations around the South, Vernon was attracted to Winston-Salem, North Carolina, for our slightly more carcinogenic and less delicious home state shame-pride of Camel cigarettes, which he harbored a fondness for.

Four years after purchasing the recipe, Vernon opened the first Krispy Kreme. Originally he sold the

Eat Like a Local

pastries to local grocery stores, but the smell from his kitchen drew in residents who wanted to buy directly out of the oven. He cut a hole directly in the wall of the factory, opening up to customers walking up from the street, originating their famous "Hot Donuts Now" drive-up concept.

Rudolph also innovated the consistency that multiple locations of the same restaurants now emulate. When he began opening new Krispy Kreme brick-and-mortars, each store made the famous donuts from scratch, which created too much variation. He solved this problem by opening a larger plant that delivered the pre-made dough to each store, and as the system improved, the company invented their own machinery that automated the entire process from the baking to the final glaze before it goes to the customer.

Today, the company which only went international less than twenty years ago boasts more than 350 United States locations and has stores in more than two dozen countries. Ten percent of its US locations are in blessed North Carolina. Surely it's unrelated that more than one out of ten adult North Carolinians have diabetes.

6. PEPSI, THE ORIGINAL COLON CLEANSE

Pepsi was invented in an eastern North Carolina pharmacy and marketed as a health drink, an interesting take given that sodas are mostly sugar and water. In 1893, Caleb Bradham started selling Brad's Drink, a digestive aid that included carbonated water, kola nuts, vanilla, and lemon. The New Bern pharmacist and health nut had a disdain for Coca Cola, which openly contained cocaine; he was a revolutionary of his time and thought it was a dangerous stimulant. The original Pepsi was stimulant-free and didn't even have caffeine.

7. CHEERWINE (AND MOONSHINE AND NASCAR)

Twenty years later on the opposite side of the state, a Salisbury man named Lewis D. Peeler bought a bottling company that sold a questionably-flavored beverage so disgusting it bankrupted the business. The delightfully toothpaste-tasting Mint Cola had to be replaced, and there was the additional challenge that sugar was rationed during World War I.

He tried sweetening his new drink with cherries, and by then people must have been a little wary of cocaine because there's no hint of it in the recipe. All

Eat Like a Local

North Carolinians remember at least one time in childhood when they got "drunk", thinking they were being naughty by drinking something with the word "wine" in the title. Sadly there's no alcohol content either; the "cheer" was decided on because Peeler felt it cheery to drink, and "wine" refers to the deep red wine-like color. Cheerwine was born.

Federal regulators as recently as 1992 investigated the company for allegedly encouraging children to consume alcohol, but the misconception hasn't harmed the Carolina Bottling Company. The cola wasn't available outside of North Carolina until around the time the Federal Bureau of Alcohol, Tobacco, and Firearms had to admit it was about as dangerous as root beer, and even then it was only expanded to Lesser Carolina (which some people know as South Carolina). In its centennial year, 2017, fellow Carolinians PepsiCo began distributing it nationwide.

The innocent fruity drink inspired by mouthwash and the wartime spirit of depriving us of joy and baked goods was produced in a former whiskey distillery though, another proud North Carolina vice. Only one county separates Rowan County, of which Salisbury is the county seat, from Wilkes County, once known as the Moonshine Capital of the World. As leading purveyors of homemade liquor, young local men would deliver the product all over the country. The product was contraband of course, and federal agents were all over the county trying to shut down the operations. This meant the drives often involved high-speed car chases down winding and steep mountain roads, the likes of which you have never seen on Los Angeles live news feeds. The dangerous driving became sport for locals and the stock-car racing that would eventually lead to the creation of NASCAR was born.

8. TEXAS PETE – NOT TEXAN AND A LITTLE RACIST

Texas has been taking credit for Texas Pete since 1929. The number three selling hot sauce in America was created at a barbecue joint (where all culinary genius is born in the state) in Winston-Salem. The creator was using a variation of the traditional western tomato-based sauce and customers asked for a little more kick, so he added cayenne peppers.

When Sam Garner, owner of the Dixie Pig, started marketing the sauce, someone suggested the name "Mexican Joe," an ever-so-tasteful ode to the heat of cuisine south of the border. The Garner family nixed that idea, but not because it was tacky. Oh no! They wanted that sauce to be American, by God, and those Texans have spicy food, too - you know, not at all because it was...Mexican? Well, the geography having been settled even if politics and American history knowledge were a tad questionable, Sam still wanted a tribute to his sons. There were three of them: Thad, Ralph, and Pete. Texas Thad wasn't very catchy, and Texas Ralph was kind of nerdy, but Texas Pete sounded like a cowboy who lived on the edge and loved hot sauce.

Thank you for the delicious racist hot sauce, Garner family.

9. BOJANGLES' V. HARDEE'S (V. NEWCOMER COOK OUT)

These fast food chains aren't so much a debate as they are sources of North Carolina clogged artery pride. Outside of North Carolina, they aren't very common, but they're expanding. Displaced North Carolinians crave this goodness and are known to make first stops upon homecomings at one or all three after leaving the airport.

"The Bo," as we shamelessly refer to Bojangles', opened in the 1970s in Charlotte and now has almost 700 locations across the eastern seaboard as far north as Pennsylvania, with almost half in North Carolina. It's famous for buttermilk biscuits, fried chicken, a cajun-seasoning french fry mix they've had to start bottling for obsessive consumers, and a sweet tea with enough sugar it appears North Carolina is trying to apologize for the World War I rationing that gave the world Cheerwine.

Then there are some people who aren't Bo biscuit people, but they will go out of their way for a Hardee's biscuit. Most of us find merits in both biscuits and hit Hardee's for burgers that don't taste like fast food. Hardee's opened about a decade and a half before Bojangles' in Greenville as a drive-in by the campus of East Carolina University, and it's a bit more well-known with several thousand locations in almost every state and more than three dozen countries. Allegedly founder Wilber Hardee lost his majority share in the restaurant bearing his name in a game of poker in 1963. He didn't like the idea of not being in charge so he sold the rest of his shares to the men who won the majority. He walked away, and he still spoke with pride in the restaurant he created until his death in 2018.

The true story is actually a little darker (and more fascinating) than that, but that's the whitewashed version. The real story is the food - gigantic charbroiled burgers that taste like they came off the backyard grill, thick milkshakes, and biscuits and sweet tea that rival Bojangles'. There are no better fast food burgers in the country.

And then there's Cook Out, distinctly delicious and founded in 1989 in Greensboro. Cook Out didn't leave North Carolina until 2010 and then it only

Eat Like a Local

ventured to Lesser Carolina, now with just over 100 in the eastern part of the country. Cook Out is a double drive-thru with an almost overwhelming menu, although everyone has a favorite, and the prices are so low it's hard to understand how they stay in business. What really makes it stand apart are its milkshakes, with over forty flavors that they'll be happy to mix and match, that cause the car lines to wrap around the building and out into very annoyed traffic.

10. MOUNT OLIVE GETS IN A PICKLE

The otherwise sleepy town of Mount Olive, North Carolina, has a thriving pickle plant that employs most of the town and is the biggest independent pickle company in the country. In the southeast, it takes seventy percent of the pickle market share. The factory has an interesting backstory, opened by a Lebanese immigrant in the 1920s as a way to reduce food waste, from the leftovers of cucumber crops from local farmers who also needed an economic boost in the poverty-ridden area.

The Mt. Olive Pickle Company is largely invested in its town and the local community, with many of the original investing families still serving on the board. In the 1970s with the aid of the United States government, it discovered a secret to the science of fermentation that helped to minimize food waste even further and improve canning processes globally.

Its history is not all rosy, though it worked out in the end. In 1998 the Farm Labor Organizing Committee (FLOC) called for a boycott until the company paid their cucumber growers better. The goal was actually to improve pay for the laborers employed by the growers, because the reimbursements to growers were so low that the workers were the ones who were cheated in the end. The union negotiated better pay and now 60% of the state's migrant workers are union-protected as a result.

There were five hard years during the boycott, living without those pickles, but now families across the state can once again ship them to expatriate children who crave the vinegary goodness that tastes like home.

11. NABS, AN UNPROVEN CONSPIRACY THEORY

These are those little crackers in plastic packaging usually sold in vending machines, and to people outside North Carolina you'd recognize them more by the current brand name Lance Crackers. There is one lovely neon square faux-cheese flavor, and a round buttery cracker, both with vague-hint-of-peanut-butter filling.

They've been around since 1913 and were then and still are headquartered in Charlotte, but we believe they may actually be a hologram created by witchcraft or that the company is a front for money laundering because no one has bought the crackers since at least 1987, when the last Generation X grandma went into a nursing home, yet they keep appearing in our purses and office desk drawers, and the company is somehow still in business. We have no evidence but there is no other rational explanation.

HOME COOKING WE TAKE CREDIT FOR

If you really want to make a friend, go to someone's house and eat with him - the people who give you their food give you their heart. - Cesar Chavez, farm organizer

12. SHRIMP AND GRITS WAS INVENTED HERE

Both shrimp and grits seem to be an acquired taste for anyone outside the Carolinas, and the combination perhaps even moreso; and while Georgia up through the Carolinas is known as the "Grits Belt", Lesser Carolina tries to take credit for the birth of shrimp and grits too. Therefore, this one is up for debate, but in the Tarheel State we double-down.

In the coastal plains of Greater Carolina, shrimp and grits is a staple and not the gourmet fine occasion plate served up in high end foodie establishments these days. Grits is an everyday food we eat with butter, salt and pepper every morning. Shrimp is pretty easy to find right off the boat and not a particular high-cost item on the coast - especially if you are the shrimper, which is the group that invented the dish in the first place. The corn served with the nutritious crustacean was ideal back in the days of heavy fishing because it's easy and fast to make and even after it cools it stays delicious, plus the grits are filling and the shrimp has all the protein one needs for a day or two of heavy work at sea.

The dish became iconic in the 1980s when the famous Crook's Corner of Chapel Hill version was raved about in the New York Times. That version includes cheese, but the beauty of the dish is in its versatility. I'm not a cheese grits fan (though I make an exception for Crook's and a few others, I concede that I'm in the minority on this, and it's the only dish on God's green earth I'd pass up cheese for) and my personal recipe is heavier on garlic and pepper. Others throw in sauteed vegetables, pimiento cheese, barbecue sauce, other meats and even other types of seafood.

13. FRIED GREEN TOMATOES ARE A DELICACY

This dish is such a common item in North Carolina that I was almost forty and craving it in a foreign country before I even realized the green tomatoes were unripened and not a special variety of tomato. I'd look for the variety everywhere, to strange looks, before I googled it and found out it was under my nose the whole time. Granted, I do not have the green thumb most North Carolians do, so this may have been common knowledge to others.

The delicacy is a sliced unripened tomato fried in buttermilk and cornmeal, with a dipping sauce that varies depending on preference but usually is a spicy remoulade. You can make it with red ripe tomatoes but they may turn out too mushy, and if they're too unripened they'll be too firm.

The dish is so traditionally Southern there has been a book and movie with it as a title, and some of us eat them like potato chips. In my house, tomatoes purchased at the green stage are never around long enough for them to turn red, which is my humble excuse for not realizing they were the same variety in the first place.

14. FORGET TOAST! WE DO BISCUITS AND GRAVY

By now it's probably well established that biscuits are an important North Carolina staple. We'll eat them with just about anything on them - meats, cheeses, fruits, and sauces. But the favorite way to consume them, if you haven't surpassed your heart attack-inducing food intake for the week, is with sausage gravy. The sauce is made with flour, milk, and pork. The recipe was born of economy, using the last scraps of meat after cooking a hearty meal, but saving money by using items found easily in the cupboard. High in calorie, fat, and protein count, it was nutritious enough to keep hard workers going when they didn't have much time for breaks.

The added bonus is that it's absolutely delicious.

15. UNLESS WE'RE IN THE MOUNTAINS WHERE WE REPLACE THE SAUSAGE WITH...CHOCOLATE

No one has a really good explanation for how this strange combination came to exist, and it's a food that one Appalachian resident will swear they've never heard of while their neighbor eats it every week and grew up with a recipe passed down through the generations.

It's a Sunday morning tradition for many families in Appalachia, and families who haven't heard the term "chocolate gravy" will often know of it as sopping chocolate. Until I was in college I denied having heard of chocolate gravy; as a half-breed mountaineer with a mother from the mountains and a father from the coast, I was only a partial expert with a foot in both worlds and thought sopping chocolate was a scrumptious sauce to dip a biscuit in, but had no idea it was used only for that or that some called it gravy.

It's made of chocolate, butter, flour, milk, and sugar. Thicker than hot fudge, whether you think it sounds crazy or not, it's chocolate in liquid form, so surely you should try it. A love for this recipe has inspired many variations, with blackberries or peaches and cream, or stewed apples, or many other sweet concoctions served over a biscuit split into two pieces.

16. WE'RE AT WAR WITH VIRGINIA AND GEORGIA ABOUT WHO INVENTED BRUNSWICK STEW

Every place has a small variation to the famous Brunswick stew, and it's the kind of smorgasbord that may vary as well based on everything in your cupboard. It's a tomato-based soup, and the North Carolina version is thicker than most with potatoes and barbecue pork added (other versions in the American South use chicken, but they are very misguided). It's also usually full of corn, okra, tomatoes, and lima beans. Some of the old folks tell you it isn't ready to eat until the paddle can stand up in the middle of the pot. It's a cold weather stew and it's filling enough to be a one-pot meal, but the truth is we'll eat it anytime and especially love it as a side dish to a giant plate of barbecue.

If you're a world traveler you might think this dish sounds familiar, and it's true. It's similar to gumbo and ratatouille, and I've tasted almost exact replicas in a couple of African countries and surprisingly in remote indigenous villages of Guatemala. But there's never been one as good as the one that comes out of Carolina kitchens, and anyone who has tried Brunswick stew will tell you the same.

17. PIMENTO CHEESE – THE BEST ANCESTRY TEST FOR NATIVE NORTH CAROLINIANS

The real MVP of this story is the pimento cheese, and we can tell if your North Carolina roots are true or if we'll allow you into the club based on two factors - "Do you make a face before trying it?" and "Did you ask if we spelled it right?" Yes, a pimento is a pimiento, and no, we don't know why the rest of you put in the pretentious, extraneous "i."

Some people not blessed to be from the South have no idea what this delicacy is. It's cheddar or hoop cheese, which is a giant hunk of cheese you can get cut off a wheel in a general store (which still exist in some small Carolina towns) and doesn't have the bite of cheddar; sometimes you can use a little of both cheeses. Add mayonnaise or cream cheese and jarred or fresh pimentos, and you have the best cheese spread of all time.

The best version comes from your grandma's kitchen, but the second best (or third after your second grandma?) is in a plastic tub from a company called Ruth's, and every North Carolinian has spent the better part of their lives with a container of it in their refrigerator. If Grandma isn't available, don't worry, because sometimes the Ruth's is sold out but every mom & pop restaurant in the state has a grandma in the kitchen who whips up an outstanding version.

The longer you're in North Carolina the more you'll find that we can work this spread into any dish, but I recommend it as a topping for burgers, a chip dip, a nacho topping, and on fries. It's a great snack with a slice of bread or crackers, but a real comfort food is with bread slapped on a grill. There is nothing better.

18. CAROLINA STYLE ANYTHING

Burgers and hot dogs are delicacies where I come from, and we love them Carolina style. That's with chili, slaw, mustard, and chopped onions. A level up

Eat Like a Local

is fondly referred to as The Heart Attack and includes bacon, cheese, and pickle relish. The Carolina style is so famous that some fast food places alter their menu to add it on within the borders of the state. Wendy's had an especially good Carolina style burger for many years and some of us were a little brokenhearted when it faded out. Some hipster and foodie establishments have started adding "Carolina style" to fries, nachos, seafood, and other bases, and much like almost every ingredient combination in our culinary traditions, they sound a little crazy but taste amazing.

19. WHERE MASHED POTATOES BECOME DESSERT

The most famous Moravian holdover is a sugar cake, which is now happily consumed year-round but is traditionally a Christmas dish. It's a coffee cake made with yeast and, oddly perhaps, mashed potatoes. That makes it very moist and the baker can form deep wells in the dough with their fingertips. Then a mixture of butter, brown sugar, and cinnamon is poured over it. Other famous Moravian dishes include chicken pies, ginger cookies, lovefeast buns (it looks like a hamburger bun but it's sweet with nutmeg, lemon juice, and orange juice - and when we aren't consuming them whole directly from Winkler's Bakery in Winston-Salem, we do use them for sandwiches), and traditional foods more commonly associated with Germany. The Moravian sugar cakes and sugar and ginger cookies can be found all over the state, but the rest is much easier to get in the west than it is in the east.

20. SANDWICH BREAD IS A LOWLY REPLICA OF A BISCUIT

We take biscuits seriously, which you've understood by now. Most commonly, we'll spread jam and butter on them, or warm a piece of cheese. We might eat one for breakfast (although they are a three meal a day kind of food) with an egg, cheese, and bacon, sausage, or country ham. But honestly, we'll put anything on a biscuit, and we'll eat them plain too. They're divine with cinnamon and a glaze, and I've eaten a few delicious burgers, barbecues, and briskets on them too. There are hundreds of restaurants known for their delicious biscuits, and we all have a favorite, but we don't start duels over the debate the way we do barbecue. You might be wrong about the best biscuit, and I respectfully sneer in your direction, but you have a right to be wrong - and I'll happily engage in a taste test.

21. BOILED PEANUTS, A STAPLE THAT SHOULD BE REMOVED

Boiled peanuts are an eastern North Carolina specialty, and I'm going to say something that may get me ex-communicated: we can't be right about everything. They're the opposite of an adage I use all the time. "Even a broken clock is right twice a day" - except this is one of the only two things we got wrong (the other is coming up). Some people will fight me over this the way other Americans brawl over pineapple on pizza, but these snacks are an example of the rare time North Carolina got food dead wrong.

It's a pretty simple recipe, and that's because it isn't hard to make something taste disgusting. You take a fresh, green, delicious peanut, grown in the finest most blessed soil on the planet, you add salt and water, and you ruin everything beautiful about it.

Still, they're worth trying once. You might be one of the people who find absolutely delicious the slimy foods that once tasted like God's grace in a hard shell but now have the flavor of broken dreams and disappointment. More likely, you'll gag and never touch another, but you'll have a greater appreciation for the all the food we got right.

22. OKRA ISN'T FROM HERE BUT IT CAN STAY

I have heard that like boiled peanuts, okra is an acquired taste, but I wouldn't know because I definitely acquired it. I might have acquired yours too, and somewhere there may be a tiny village of people wondering who acquired their taste for okra - it's here; I have all of them, and I won't give them back. There is no sign that shouts quite so loudly "You're home!" as driving past a field of okra in the late summer, with eight foot tall plants topped in buttery yellow flowers and okra pods pointing proudly up to the sun.

No one is really sure where okra originated; it could be Asia, India, or Africa, but it definitely wasn't in a North Carolina field. I don't really mind where it started as long as it ends up in my belly, and the only real problem I've found is that no one ever makes enough of it at one time. Southerners really love a good fried okra, and kind of like the boiled peanut misstep, there are a few wayward souls who love a good slimy boiled okra. I'm going to tell you though that the best way to eat okra is the easiest - raw.

This is the way Carolina children whose grandparents were farmers grew up eating it in clandestine, ruining the summer crops by sneaking into the fields and popping it right off the plant. It's a sweet fond memory but perhaps a little toxic. My cousins and I were banned from the fields for a few years when my grandmother, in the childlike phase of her descent into Alzheimer's disease, would join us for our contraband snacks but then went into acute liver failure. She ratted out all of her poor innocent little descendents when the doctor blamed her condition on eating unrinsed okra that still likely had pesticides on it (oh calm down, she recovered).

Remember kids, rinse your produce. Also, there are many organic okras available these days and pesticides are safer than back in those days - don't let my sweet reminiscing of organ failures and senility scare you.

23. FRIED COLLARDS, A SUPERFOOD – KIND OF

Collards are another acquired taste plant supposedly, but who knows if that's really true because everyone here consumes them almost as much as oxygen. It's probably the food most distinguishable as being a "Southern" food you'll be hard pressed to find served elsewhere in the country, though I find them more and more in the hipster restaurants that pop up throughout the country and make Southern food seem quaint. (I sneer but secretly I'm delighted with it if it means I get to eat like home all around the country).

Collards, also known as "greens" or "collard greens" and similar but also not anything like turnips or spinach, grow like little green bouquets in the fields, a sight that makes me smile and think of Carolina no matter what part of the world I'm in when I see it.

The North Carolina way to make collards is to take the superfood and make it as unhealthy as possible, boiling it with salt, ham, bacon drippings, potatoes, and red peppers, until you've cooked out all of the nutrients it could possibly have left in it and the tough leaf is so deliciously delicate it will practically melt in your mouth. Then you douse it to taste with red pepper vinegar, but most North Carolinians believe if you haven't come close to making a thick collard stew with vinegar base, it isn't "to taste" enough.

The juice left in the pot is called pot liquor, or "likker" depending on who is spelling it out, and it is a Carolina nectar of the gods, best enjoyed sopped up with cornbread and more than once just devoured directly from the pot by this writer. Supposedly it's an aphrodisiac as well, which is a strange and awkward thing to consume with such ravenousness in front of your family, so when I'm stealing the pot liquor I try to distract everyone with decoys in another direction.

Eat Like a Local

24. LIVING IN SIN

Deviled eggs aren't particularly evil; in fact they're downright angelic and the life of every party in which a Southerner is required to bring a covered dish. "Deviled" usually means a food has been made spicy in some way, and that can be applied to this favored snack - boiled eggs cut in half with the yolk mixed with some variation that usually includes mayonnaise, mustard, salt, pepper, and sometimes a dash of vinegar or pickle relish. The kick can be leveled up a notch with paprika.

This is a get-together snack that might be the only way one person can consume a dozen eggs without even realizing what they've done. They're guaranteed to be at any event, and I usually go straight to the food table and seek them out. I serve them at parties in every country I've ever traveled and people stare at me like I've lost my mind until I convince revelers to try them, and then the plate disappears and people begin requesting them at every event I attend.

25. LIVERMUSH (AND OTHER WEIRD MEATS)

North Carolina is most famous for its barbecue, but it has a long, proud, and sometimes baffling history of other and weirder meats too. First let's get the strange unnecessarily red hot dogs out the way - Bright Leaf hot dogs are an eastern NC staple beef and pork sausage with a peppery taste that gives many people pause due to the red additives. That makes them stand out (apart from their imitators) but the brand actually has less additives and preservatives than other hot dogs on the market, are sold fresh, and don't last long on the shelf, which is fine because they go pretty fast to the belly anyway. The brand also makes almost as famous Red Hots, which are shorter and fatter and even spicier. Enjoy them just like a hot dog.

In tobacco country in eastern North Carolina, we make an air-dried country sausage that brings out the pork taste in a sharp and savory way. The unique flavor comes from the air exposure, and each place has slightly different recipes depending on the spice blends, but my favorites come out of Martin County.

There I grew up with a neighbor to my grandparents who sold his sausage to chain grocery stores throughout northeastern North Carolina but brought over a cooler of it to gift my grandfather when he heard I was coming to visit from my native Wilmington, which was sadly about an hour south of

Eat Like a Local

the southernmost grocery store he served. He knew his was my favorite, and to this day though he is no longer living his family still uses the same recipe, and I stock up with enough to last for months whenever I go to visit.

When you're in northeastern North Carolina, hit the meat section of the local grocery stores and get as much Griffin's Sausage as your freezer, wallet, and shopping buggy can handle. (A "shopping buggy" is a grocery cart to you Yankees - and "you Yankees" is what we call anyone from north of North Carolina or west of middle Tennessee, a term of endearment if we say it to your face).

Then there's country ham. The history on this food is traced back to our general area but specifically close over the state line in Virginia. It's heavily salted and cured and smoked, a preservation method invented to keep it from spoiling in the Southern heat in the era before refrigeration. And yes, we condescendingly refer to deli cold-cut ham (which we also consume in large voracious quantities) as "city ham."

Finally, we have liver pudding and livermush. In my world, no one knows who actually eats it, but somewhere there exists a shady underworld that feeds off of it. Is your stomach feeling strong? If not, skip ahead. Liver pudding, found mostly in the east, is boiled pork liver and trimmings, then grinded with coarse cornmeal added. Livermush is the western

43

version, made with finer cornmeal. The pudding is cut into blocks and while livermush is as well, it's then pan fried or served on bread. Somehow these dishes are so popular that North Carolina is actually forced to claim them.

26. BILL FRIDAY'S PEANUT BRITTLE

Every native North Carolinian considers Bill Friday a celebrity, even if outsiders have never heard of him. He was President of the University of North Carolina school system for three decades in its heyday that made it a truly great institution, and four decades as host of a show called North Carolina People on the public access channel UNC-TV. The show overlapped by only a few years his time as President; Friday continued to the show until his death at age 92 in 2012.

Peanut brittle is a famous Southern candy and North Carolinians all have recipes, but his is special as a regional favorite. He loved gift-giving so much that every year during the holidays he made 75 pounds of it, and if you were a recipient you were officially one of the cool kids. As far as I know my family never got any directly, but I recall tasting a small sampling of Mr. Friday's personal peanut brittle more than once from some of the people whose circles intersected in the Venn diagram of social echelons in the state. Even in a world of outstanding peanut brittle, his was divine.

Dr. Friday insisted on peanuts from a particular mill, A&B Milling of Enfield, and as granddaughter of a peanut farmer and miller who was a close competitor, I agree that every mill definitely manages to produce their own unique taste. He only put in just enough candy to hold the peanuts together, and combined the peanuts with butter, sugar, and corn syrup, in a recipe that was borrowed from his wife's family and they've now generously shared with the world so that we can all have Dr. Friday's delicious candy even after his passing.

27. THE MOST HUMBLE PIE

The rest of the country lives for pumpkin pie every Thanksgiving, but in North Carolina where sweet potato crops reign supreme, we take out the pumpkin and add in our state's number one crop. Most family tables will actually offer up both options, but the sweet potato disappears first. In other homes, if there's only one option, it's usually the native pride dish.

This is another example of African-American adaptations of native culinary traditions, as yams of a different variety are a staple native to African soils. First recipes were more savory dishes, but it evolved to the dessert we are most familiar with today.

Personally at the Thanksgiving table, I'm the rare defector who chooses pumpkin pie over the North Carolina favorite, but I love sweet potatoes in just about any other dish, and as a comfort food every other time of year, sweet potato pie is a go-to especially if it's infused with bourbon and candied pecans - more favored North Carolina ingredients.

28. THE MOST UNNATIVE NATIVE FOOD OF ALL TIME

Banana pudding isn't necessarily a North Carolina invention, and bananas obviously aren't native plants, but it is practically a part of our own food special group, which we call Pig Pickin' and is comprised of course of barbecue and its complements.

The fine dessert can be thrown together in five minutes with boxed vanilla pudding, branded 'Nilla wafer cookies, canned whipped cream, and bananas, that every Southerner keeps on hand for times on crisis in which a fast and sweet comfort food is required, or you can go all out with homemade vanilla wafers and custard, and a meringue or whipped cream you throw together yourself. We love them all and we

Eat Like a Local

aren't picky. These four ingredients blended together are simply a perfect combination of pleasure that we have every time we eat barbecue, any time we get together with family or for other special occasions, and, frankly, any time we have all the supplies on hand, which is always.

29. SONKER OR COBBLER?

Very naive people will claim a sonker is another word for cobbler (which is also a beloved dessert in North Carolina and throughout the South), but native western North Carolinians know better, even if this daughter of a baker did grow up confused and thought they were both called "conkers". In my defense, I'm not the only one - a friend raised in sonkerlandia once told me that in elementary school the first time he heard the word "conquerors" in Social Studies class, he thought they were bakers until he went home and told his parents about bakers taking over the world and their subjects merrily eating sugared fruity pastries.

Sonker is mostly a specialty in Surry and Wilkes Counties (yes, the same county that brought us moonshine and NASCAR, those blessed folks), and it's like a cobbler but deeper and juicier, with very ripe fruit just before it goes bad and often with a sweet dipping sauce served on the side. Kind of like biscuits with chocolate gravy, people from outside of Surry and Wilkes Counties are likely to have never heard of sonker, although thanks to Surry's annual Sonker Festival and the blessing of the internet, that is changing.

Surry doesn't have much else in the way of tourism except for its claim to fame with Mt. Airy being the inspiration for Mayberry in The Andy Griffith Show, but these days it even has a Sonker Trail, which includes stops at restaurants best known for the delicacy - the ones I can vouch for are Southern on Main and Roxxi & Lulu's both of Elkin, Putter's Patio and Grill of Dobson, The Living Room in Pilot Mountain, and three stops in Mount Airy called Down Home Restaurant, Old North State Winery, and Miss Angel's Heavenly Pies (which is my favorite thanks to the moonshine content). That list is always changing, so before you head out on the Sonker Trail, go in person to the Mount Airy Visitor's Center to get the latest list.

FUN FOOD FACTS

After a good dinner, one can forgive anybody, even one's own relatives. - Oscar Wilde, writer

30. WEIRD & DELICIOUS FOOD FESTIVALS

I once read an article called 10 Can't Miss Food Festivals in North Carolina, or something to that effect, and I was surprised, because I can't imagine limiting that list to ten. For three hours, I struggled to limit my list to thirty! For the sake of space, I then closed my eyes and randomly deleted ten more, which upon reflection may be how that other food writer got their list whittled down.

This is divided up by month, and I skipped entirely November through March. There are a few great festivals in that time, but the list is already long, and let's be honest, unless they're mountain folks, North Carolinians don't enjoy leaving the house if it's going to be below 60 degrees outside.

April

Newport Annual Pig Cookin'

America's largest whole hog barbecue, this is some of the most fun I have all year. Sixty cooks come from around the region and you can try as many of them as you can handle, at $7 a heaping plate. I try to go with a big group of friends and we all get two, and everyone takes a bite.

Grifton- Grifton Annual Shad Festival

Shad is a rich-tasting herring and the festival is one of the largest and longest-running in the state. A celebration of a river fish seems like a weird base for a festival, and Grifton is a town you might not otherwise explore. This makes for a delightfully eccentric event you should experience at least once. The first time I went was because I thought it was a shag dance festival; I was surprised but the event was enough fun that I've been back a few times.

Asheville- Artisan Bread Bakers' Festival

A bit calmer than most festivals, but full of workshops and delicious baked items from famous and local bakers. I enjoy this one and come home with breads and pastries I'd never seen before.

Eat Like a Local

Mount Olive- North Carolina Pickle Festival

There are only so many pickles one person can eat at a time, I always thought, until I saw a pickle-eating contest at this festival. There's also a pickle derby and people dressed as pickles, which should be odd but apparently isn't.

May

ChadbournStrawberry Festival

There are a few strawberry festivals, but Chadbourn is the Strawberry Capital of the World and gets the official state designated event. It's also the largest and oldest agricultural festival in the state. The celebration brings about 10,000 people a year, which is ten times the actual population of the town. This festival is held about an hour from my hometown, and if I'm home I try to never miss it. Strawberries are my favorite food and the food contest is the highlight of the entire month of May.

Kinston- Barbecue Festival on The Neuse

This is the largest barbecue cook-off in North Carolina. That's different from April's largest barbecue in general because this one is a contest. This event has 90 participants and you can eat barbecue and drink beer and wine all day, trying to stay upright to manage your children.

Asheville- Herb Festival

Oh Asheville! Another one of those refined and fancy festivals. This one has every herb you can imagine and many cool workshops for cooking and crafts with herbs. I learned how to make my own essential oils and soaps here, and the years I have gone I have been able to stock up on herbs that I can't find elsewhere in North Carolina.

Smithfield- Ham & Yam Festival

Sweet potatoes and yams are different crops but we use the terms interchangeably for no good reason, and we're actually referring to sweet potatoes here. There's also a barbecue cook-off here but generally after two big barbecue events and all the ham and sweet potatoes, I skip that part. I know, it's hard to believe.

Elizabeth City- NC Potato Festival

There are unlimited free french fries here, which is the most important thing. Get there at 10 AM so you can gorge yourself before they run out. I

Eat Like a Local

take this very seriously. They run out at least an hour before they planned on the years I attend because of how many I have packed into my purse. There's also a potato peeling contest, which I watch very intently to see if anyone loses a finger but thus far I've been let down.

June

Burgaw- Blueberry Festival

Thirty thousand people attend this festival every year and it's one of my favorites, one near my hometown that I attend as often as possible. Like almost all festivals, we have a barbecue cook-off and a craft beer garden, and naturally there is a baking contest and everything blueberry you can possibly eat.

July

Grandfather MountainHighland Games

I grew up attending this festival with my mother and her parents, and it's a fun and unusual experience you definitely won't get growing up everywhere, but you can't get much whiter without a hate crime.

Here they celebrate the Scottish heritage of many of the area settlers, and there are a multitude of bagpipes and men in kilts unironically. In terms of food you can try traditional Scottish foods and Appalachian fare as well. The whiskey tasting starts two hours before the sheep herding, which I think makes the second event even more fun.

There are some amazing harp and fiddle demonstrations and competitions, and the most fascinating part is the "heavy athletics" portion, where contestants throw heavy objects, the most unbelievable of which is a tall log, a contest called "turning the caber."

Lenoir- Blackberry Festival

Lenoir is a fun little town in the western part of the state, and this is a great time to take a weekend to explore while eating everything blackberry you can imagine. There is a Blackberry Brigade, which is actually one of the cutest parades you'll ever see, right out of a Disney film, with little ones in costumes pulling wagons of blackberries. This is one of my favorite festivals all year.

Eat Like a Local

Candor- Peach Festival

This is pretty much the same as all the other fruit festivals, with peaches. I love the baking competitions here and it's the best peach ice cream out of a whole lot of very good peach ice cream I've ever tasted.

August

Sneads Ferry Shrimp Festival

As much shrimp as you can stand to eat, and plenty of other good food vendors too, with some of the best country and bluegrass live shows you'll see at any festival all year in the state.

Black Mountain Sourwood Festival

This festival is all about honey and bees, and 30,000 people attend every year in this gorgeous small town outside of Asheville.

September

Ayden Collard Festival

The official state collard festival, because somewhere there is another one. This is the same small town that hosts two of the best barbecue restaurants in the state, and one of them, Bum's, donates all the collards for the annual collard eating contest. If you've tasted those collards, you know entry is a hot-ticket item. This is a fun day event for the family.

Oxford Hot Sauce Contest

This event not far from Raleigh is pretty new and already draws 15,000 people a year. Started as a way to promote local food products, it took off and exceeded expectations. The hot sauce contest isfun to participate in and of course there is plenty of barbecue to taste test it on, with a pepper eating contest that is both hilarious and scary to watch. Every year I, a hot sauce connoisseur, buy so many bottles of the stuff at this event that there is no need to purchase any others until the next year rolls around.

October

Shelby Livermush Festival

I am as shocked as you are that anyone celebrates this. More surprisingly, it's the second of the year, with a June event in Marion. This one is the bigger of the two and where it's easier to gawk at the weirdos who enjoy the food while eating safe festival foods like bacon and Sun Drop from a distance. There is a brew festival and a chili cook-off, an adorable dog costume contest, and a Miss Livermush beauty pageant, which is actually a coveted title.

Morehead City Seafood Festival

Hands down this is the most delicious festival of the year, and it's a tough month to survive with so many good festivals that include this one and the state fair too. It's in a beautiful place too, and other than the eating, my favorite part is the blessing of the fleet, when all the boats pass. There's great music at this festival too.

Mount Airy Sonker Festival

This is a very small festival, but it's a great time to go up and try all the sonkers on and off the Sonker Trail and explore the area in its prettiest time of year. They have good bluegrass music and Appalachian flat foot dancing exhibitions as well.

North Wilkesboro Brushy Mountain Apple Festival

There are at least three apple festivals in North Carolina but this is the biggest and best with 160,000 attendees. That's three times the population of the entire county (which if you'll recall is the same county that brought us moonshine and NASCAR, so you know they have fun at this festival). Just like the Mount Airy festival that is usually the same weekend, this is the most gorgeous time of year to explore the area, and they're less than an hour from one another. Take a weekend and see Mount Airy the first day and Wilkes County the next.

Raleigh North Carolina State Fair

I lose my mind at the North Carolina State Fair and become a screaming redneck at the demolition derby, embarrassing my children until they forget their composure too and start behaving like me. I don't ride any rides because most of them terrify me, but while my kids enjoy them I stand below and pray for their safety while stuffing my face with the ridiculous foods the fair is offering for the year.

The people who come up with these things are monsters and I want to be on the state fair food committee, which may not be a real thing, so I can be the one to taste test it all and just wildly approve whatever insanity is presented before me. Fruity Pebble bacon? You're in. Deep-fried oreos, glad to see you back. Krispy Kreme Texas Pete mini-donuts? "Mini" is the only thing you got wrong on that one! A "crack-n-cheese" waffle cone, you say? With mac-n-cheese, turkey barbecue, cracklings, coleslaw, and some kind of mystery sauce I probably don't want to know about - and no actual crack? Send. Me. Three.

Deep-fried Jell-O, bacon pimento cheeseburger eggrolls, the "Man Sandwich" (which is a grilled cheese wrapped in bacon which I assure you this woman can handle), and what may be the greatest invention in the 21st century, chicken & waffle kebabs? Are all state fairs like this or just mine? It's truly magical.

Even if I am living internationally I try to fly home in October for the state fair, and everyone knows I can't come to any events in September and I have to choose between Thanksgiving and Christmas. Sorry I miss your September birthday every year Dad, sorry I can't attend one of the large family get-togethers, I'm not the one who planned the absolutely necessary state fair right in the middle.

31. FISH CAMPS ARE BETTER THAN MICHELIN STARS

Fish camps sound like a cool place youthful fish gather in the summertime to play games, swim, and make macaroni crafts to take home to mommy and daddy fish. The reality is even better. Instead, it's a locally-owned restaurant, usually a pretty divey kind of place, that serves plates piled high with fried seafood. "Sea" food is misleading in a coastal state that is also pretty wide but full of rivers - the fish camps can be found all throughout the state and serve up fresh riverfood caught fresh and taken directly to the restaurant.

Some say that there are more fish camps in Gaston County than in the rest of the state combined, but I'm not aware of any official numbers. What I do know is that the fish camps are closely tied to textile mills, which makes sense because they're both located on rivers, and Gaston County was once the epicenter of the textile industry, which was big throughout the rest of the state as well.

On Sundays, millworkers would use their day off to go down to the river and fish. Often they'd cook up their lunch right there. This turned into shacks built on the riverbanks where the fish would be served up to visitors. Fish camps spread through the state.

Modern fish camps don't look like the originals; these days they might still be on the lower end of the luxury scale and I like to think some of the grime just adds spice to the food. However, they are (usually, definitely not always) registered restaurants inspected by the state, have indoor structures, and industrial-grade fryers these days. They're still called fish camps though and they still have the charm we imagine those old shacks did.

If you're visiting North Carolina and want to try a fish camp, just about any of them are delicious, but the best are still found along the riverbanks. Some of the best are found in the western part of the state - in

Eat Like a Local

the east, closer to the coast, we have plenty of fish camps but they get overshadowed by more formal seafood restaurants. However, in the east, one of the best fish camps I've ever tried is the Washington Crab and Seafood Shack, in the charming river town of Washington, locally called "Little Washington" and sometimes "Original Washington," because founded in 1776, it was the first city named after General George Washington. The Cypress Grill, not far away from Little Washington in the small town of Jamesville, is a close runner-up, and many will passionately declare that it far exceeds the Washington contender. It's harder to find though, and has seasonal hours. Recently closed after massive hurricane flooding, it has since reopened, answering the prayers of locals who thought the mainstay could have been gone forever. An example of what you'd imagine the originals looked like, it's located directly on the river.

32. ODDLY SPECIFIC STATE FOODS

North Carolina is indecisive about which food to declare the state food. We're problem solvers though! So we made strawberries the state red berry, blueberries the state blue berry, the Scuppernong grape the state fruit, the sweet potato the state vegetable, and milk the state drink.

33. MORE TURKEYS THAN PEOPLE

Something we proudly recite every year at Thanksgiving is that we're a national leader in turkey production - only Minnesota beats us out. Our top agricultural industry is poultry and Butterball is headquartered in Garner. The wild turkey is native to this area and Native Americans introduced British settlers to the meat, which later became a Thanksgiving staple. And yes - there are many people in North Carolina, the ninth most populous US state as of the 2016 Census, but there are three times as many turkeys. Every fourth Thursday of November, we give thanks for another year without a turkey uprising.

34. ALMOST HALF OF AMERICA'S SWEET POTATOES ARE GROWN IN EASTERN NC

If you're wondering when I'm going to stop mentioned sweet potatoes, the answer is probably never, because North Carolina grows more sweet potatoes than any other state in the country. In fact, most of them actually come from a very small area of the state in the coastal plains. We'll eat sweet potatoes with anything and prepared just about any way possible, and we probably sound a bit like Bubba Gump with his shrimp obsession in the movie Forrest Gump. You can make baked sweet potatoes, fried sweet potatoes, boiled sweet potatoes, grilled sweet potatoes, mashed sweet potatoes, candied sweet potatoes, sweet potato casserole, sweet potato pie, sweet potato fries, sweet potato soup, sweet potato ice cream, sweet potato curry, sweet potato stir fry, sweet potato milkshakes...

35. THE LARGEST PORK DISPLAY SOMEWHERE

North Carolina is the second largest producer of pork in the nation. The majority of our 2,000 hog farms are in the eastern part of the state, which makes our interstates smell amazing. When I was a girl, I passed a billboard on the way to my grandparents' house that boasted of The Largest Pork Display In The World! in Nahunta, North Carolina. I assumed this would be an artistic sculpture made of pork, which my father would never take me to.

As an adult I was disappointed to find out it was a market of every kind of pork you can imagine, and it must smell truly horrific inside, like the interstate except it's all already dead and there's no airflow. It's a gigantic building that much like my father I don't know that I want to enter, but these days it advertises as The Largest Pork Display In The Eastern United States!, which makes me very morbidly curious about who has surpassed them.

36. WE MAKE WINE AND FRY A LOT OF REALLY BIG THINGS

The world's largest producer of Muscadine wines is the Duplin Winery in eastern North Carolina. It's also the oldest winery in the American South. It's in a little town called Rose Hill which doesn't have much else as its claim to fame other than the World's Largest Frying Pan, which is only six blocks away from the winery. When I was a child I didn't know much about wine but I was a fan of Muscadine grapes, which I'd eat off my grandfather's vines. I loved going to the winery's annual grape stomp and then I'd wander up to the still functional and sometimes used frying pan, which sits in a public town square, where I'd stare into it and imagine all the things I'd fry in my frying pan when I grew up and could buy one that big.

Eat Like a Local

37. REALLY OLD WINE

The oldest cultivated grapevine in America is on Roanoke Island in the Outer Banks of North Carolina. Neither locals nor scientists know if it's native to the area or if it may have been transplanted by colonists from a British species that hasn't survived nearly as heartily, but the Scuppernong (also known as Muscadine) is now at least 400 years old and likely fed the original colonists if they weren't the cultivists. Most grapevines only live about 100 years, while this one continues to bear fruit like a Biblical figure living miraculously beyond life expectancy.

WHERE TO EAT

You don't need a silver fork to eat good food. - Paul Prudhomme, chef

38. ASHLEY'S DYNASTY

Ashley Christensten is a Raleigh-based chef who has won several prestigious awards, including in 2019 the James Beard Outstanding Chef award. I would say she owns a ridiculous amount of restaurants, except I only want her to open more. In 2007, she opened her first; Poole's Diner is one of my favorite North Carolina eateries serving classic comfort foods. In 2011, she opened three more restaurants in an old Piggly Wiggly (an iconic North Carolina grocery chain that have now mostly shuttered) - Beasley's Chicken + Honey with some of the best fried chicken and Southern side dishes you'll ever taste, Fox Liquor Bar with craft cocktails and beers (with her own incredible take on traditional bar snacks), and Chuck's serving phenomenal burgers and fries. Four years later she opened Death & Taxes, an upscale place where everything is cooked using wood fire, and Bridge Club, a private event space and cooking classroom.

If you do the math, this means that thank the heavens, it's about time for her to open up two or three more restaurants. True to the formula, Poole'side Pies, a pizza joint, is scheduled to open any day now right next to (can you tell?) her original Poole's Diner. Once you taste her food, if you can't get enough, pick up her cookbook, the bestselling Poole's: Recipes and Stories from a Modern Diner.

39. HUNTERS...BUT VEGAN

You might not have guessed by now, but I'm not vegan. I'm not even vegetarian. I sneer at salads and lean toward foods covered in gravy. But that doesn't

Eat Like a Local

mean I don't know good vegan food, and North Carolina has some of the best vegan and vegetarian restaurants in the world.

One of my very favorite restaurants is Fiction Kitchen in Raleigh. In fact, one of my favorite barbecue plates is the vegan jackfruit-based one here, and I happen to be a chicken and waffles connoisseur as well, and their's is one of the best, even if they do put the word "mock" in front of the word "chicken" on the menu. I crave their vegan "cheese" plate when I'm not in Raleigh.

Another great vegan restaurant is plant in Asheville. The eatery has things on the menu I can't pronounce, but I've tried everything they serve and I can't stop. I have literally driven six hours from my home to eat at plant. Once the carrot cake made me cry, and they have two drinks, the Red Chile Esmerita and the Sageminded, that I dream about.

Bean started in Charlotte but now has a location in Asheville too, and I can't get enough of their "crab" dip, made with jackfruit. They also serve an old-fashioned meatloaf and a Carolina burger that are completely vegan and out of this world.

The Remedy Diner in Raleigh serves a few meat dishes but is mostly known for its vegan and vegetarian cuisine. I've never actually even tried their meat dishes because the others are so delicious and I can eat like a carnivore almost everywhere else.

Everyone knows not to try to sneak anything off my plate here because my ex-husband still bears the scars from when I impulsively stabbed his hand with a fork while trying to take the last pimento cheese fry (the incident surprisingly had nothing to do with the demise of the marriage). I once made 26 sopapilla cheesecakes in a month while trying to make a copycat of theirs; after 26 I decided I was close enough but I never quite mastered it.

40. BARBECUE JOINTS

Quite obviously North Carolina is blessed with some of the best barbecue restaurants there are. Go to any town, find a local, and ask which places are best - it won't be hard. But the ones that rise above in the entire state - even those are legion.

Buxton Hall. This one is a standalone rarity because while it's located in western Asheville, it serves eastern-style barbecue. The award-winner was also voted North Carolina's best barbecue by Southern Living in 2019. While it's my current favorite barbecue joint in the state, it's a little different because most places are country mom & pop style places, and this one has a more hipster feel. It's owned by a chef from South Carolina, where mustard-based barbecue reigns supreme (it's no Eastern NC style, but reserve your doubts until you

Eat Like a Local

try it - sounds strange but it's delicious); and a self-taught chef educated first as a businessman who grew up in India and owns seven restaurants, three in very lucky Asheville.

Red Bridges Barbecue Lodge. The namesake of this Shelby, NC relic first opened more than seventy years ago and it's been going strong ever since. In 2019, it won a USA Today competition for best barbecue in North Carolina. The current owners are the grandchildren of the original, Mr. Red Bridges himself, and they took it over from their mother. In Shelby, they favor the ketchup vinegar-based style of barbecue and that's what you'll find here.

Lexington Barbecue. Located in, you guessed it, Lexington, this place might be referred to by locals as The Monk or The Honeymonk, after its founder, Wayne Monk. This place has been there for more than fifty years, serves Western-syle barbecue, and has repeatedly won national awards.

Stamey's. Stamey's in Greensboro can take credit for The Monk because Wayne Monk held one of his first jobs there and learned how to make barbecue under the tutelage of Mr. Stamey himself. Stamey's will be ninety years old in 2020 and is another western-style gem.

Bum's vs. Skylight Inn - Located in tiny out of the way Ayden, North Carolina, these eastern-style joints have a friendly rivalry. With a town population of only 5,000, they're blessed to have some of the best barbecue in the state, home to both Bum's and the Skylight Inn. Skylight Inn is the senior by a few decades but even Bum's has been around for more than forty years. They're both family affairs with generations of the founder's family continuing to work and help run the places. You'll find people who swear to one place or the other, and then there's the rest of us, who go back and forth and sing the praises of both. Bum's is a little hard to find but you can smell your way from the downtown area - literally just roll down your window and follow the smell of barbecue. Both are well known to be some of the best barbecue around and people drive from all over eastern North Carolina to Ayden to grab some for lunch.

Honestly, they prove the old adage that competition makes you better and there's room for everyone - both joints are flourishing in a town with a population roughly the size of some high schools.

41. MORE DONUTS

There's a real donut war in North Carolina, and no one is quite sure how it happened, as North Carolina isn't particularly known for round pastries with holes cut in the center until Krispy Kreme came along and we all know now that came by way of New Orleans

Eat Like a Local

and Kentucky. We're very blessed though, and it's a war we'll happily fight and not even try to settle the matter.

First there's Britt's Donuts, opened in Carolina Beach two years after Krispy Kreme's humble beginnings. It's been around for eighty years and unlike its predecessor it never had to diversify; Britt's only sells one thing - fried glazed donuts, with a line so long when they open for the season in March that it frequently wraps down the street and if you don't get there early, they run out. Britt's is almost always on national top ten donut lists in the country.

Often it's the only North Carolina place - but not always. Duck Donuts is a newcomer on the scene, founded in 2006 on the Outer Banks (in the town of Duck). Claiming to be the fastest growing donut shop in the country, it now boasts more than eighty stores after beginning to franchise in 2013. Duck Donuts is anything but a one-item menu kind of place, with made to order snacks. They have a base of a vanilla cake donut and you can add whatever toppings you like. There are eleven coatings, seven toppings (including bacon!), and four drizzles.

Founded by transplanted Pennsylvanians, they really took on the artery-clogging spirit of our proud Carolina culinary traditions by adding breakfast sandwiches and sundaes to the menu - here you can have a donut appetizer with a donut sandwich with bacon, egg, cheese, and hot sauce (with another glaze and crumbled bacon on top, if you'd like); then you can top it off with a donut covered in ice cream and another topping.

Then there's Monuts, Durham's favorite donut spot, which offers much more than donuts. The donut menu changes up daily but they offer both cake and yeast styles, with my favorites being blackberry basil, ginger fig, and maple bacon bourbon. They also have fabulous coffee and biscuits, and I've tried their entire menu and love it all. I'm a sucker for their pimento cheese and bacon bagel and the blueberry poptart.

42. SEAFOOD

Coastal North Carolina, and inland too, thanks to our plentiful lakes and rivers, is quite known for delicious pescatarian meals. It's hard to narrow down to favorites, but just a few to try include:

Outer Banks Boil Company, in Corolla and Kitty Hawk, with newer projects in Carolina Beach and now in Maryland and Delaware too, with franchise opportunities coming soon. They serve up low-country boils, a South Carolina tradition they let us borrow, and they don't have a sit-down location, but you can grab your food to-go (although you have to prepare it yourself), or have them bring the party to

Eat Like a Local

you for parties of ten or more. A low-country seafood boil is a heaven-sent concoction of jumbo shrimp, andouille sausage, potatoes, corn on the cob, and Vidalia onions, seasoned and boiled (best in water, beer, or white wine). You can make it fancier with snow crab, mussels, clams, and they offer lobster tails too. When the food is ready, it's literally just dumped on the table and you pick off what you want.

Harbor House Seafood Market in Hatteras. At Harbor House you can pick up raw fresh seafood to take back to the house or you can buy prepared to go. They make divine shrimp in Old Bay seasoning, crab legs, New England clam chowder, seafood bisque, and a seafood enchilada that I think about whenever I'm not on the island. Their hushpuppies are some of the best in all of North Carolina.

Ceviche's in Wilmington. This is a Panamanian inspired restaurant and having spent most of my non-North Carolina life in Latin America, I go here when I need a ceviche fix. Ceviche, which isn't the only thing on the menu by far but certainly the focal point, is a seafood dish of tropical fruits, onions, peppers, and seasonings, and it's technically raw but the acidic juices cook the fish. It's certainly not traditional Carolina cooking, but in a place where seafood and spices run supreme (and in a beach town where there are lots of hangovers, for which ceviche is a perfect cure), it blends in beautifully.

Dockside N' Duck Seafood Market in Duck. Similar to Harbor House in Hatteras, you can pick up fresh seafood here or ask them to steam it, and then they offer delicious premade sides and desserts for you to add on. My favorite menu items are the artichoke crab dip, the tomato pie (especially the tomato pie), and their five fruit pie. Similar to the Outer Banks Boil Company, you can also purchase steamer pots, which include all the ingredients you need and a customized choice of seafood, complete with the boiler pot.

Cape Fear Seafood Company in Wilmington and Leland. This place has inarguably one of the best shrimp & grits plates in North Carolina (yes, the grits have cheese), and I always order the Blood Mary oyster appetizer. My favorite plates are the saltimbocca and New Bedford scallops, and if you feel like the menu is a little too high-end for you, don't worry; they have great fish tacos, burgers, and salads, too.

Sunny Side Oyster Bar in Williamston. Williamston is a little town with nothing, absolutely nothing, except this oyster bar, another couple of mom & pop country cooking gems, and a giant horse showing arena. I would probably not even know about this treasure except for the fact that my family hails from this map dot. If you're not from this general area, you likely wouldn't pass through, but you could make a day of one of the horse shows with participants who come from all over the region and sometimes the

Eat Like a Local

country, by eating lunch at a little joint up the road called Griffin's Quick Lunch (which is my favorite restaurant in all of the United States and only has missed a mention otherwise here because I wouldn't know where to fit it in, in the middle of nowhere and featuring giant plates of country cooked deliciousness for under ten bucks), heading back to your horse show, and then having dinner at Sunny Side. It's been open since 1935, and you sit at a bar while the staff brings you buckets and buckets of seafood. The Sunny Side sauce is poured out of a simmering pot and the horseradish sauce will make your eyes water. They're only open in months with an R (traditionally the only months with good oysters available), so don't plan the trip unless it's September through April.

43. ASHEVILLE

Biscuit Head. Arguably the best biscuits in North Carolina. My favorites are the pulled pork, the mimosa fried chicken, and the fried green tomato biscuits.

Table. A Southern-based restaurant with a menu that changes with the seasons. I have a fondness for their nectarine appetizer, the salad with blueberry creme fraiche, and the Afghan tomatoes. For brunch they have a French toast that my daughter has driven across the state for.

Rhubarb. "Contemporary Appalachian cuisine" is how this restaurant bills its menu, and it changes weekly based on availability of ingredients. The fare is exactly as stated, traditional foods with a modern twist, and I am a fan of their pimento cheese served in a mason jar and their local cheese plates, which you can count on just about always being on the menu. Last time I was there I had the rhubarb-glazed duck confit, and Food & Wine magazine swears you should try the goat cheese burrata.

44. CHAPEL HILL

Crook's Corner. This place has Southern food on lock. I've already mentioned it here at least once, but besides shrimp & grits, you can't go wrong with the picnic plate or the pork tenderloin. I have been known to skip dinner entirely and order three desserts - it's up to you what you'd try if you're up to my challenge, but I love the Mt. Airy Chocolate Souffle Cake, banana pudding, and the Atlantic Beach Lemon-Lime Pie, which I sometimes trade out for the Frozen Mint Julep (mint sorbet with a shot of Wild Turkey) if I've had a particularly bad day.

Sunrise Biscuit Kitchen. Biscuits so good they ship nationwide. At Sunrise Biscuits they don't get crazy with the ingredients. They don't need to. It's just the normal ingredients you can order anywhere, but better. I'm a fan of their cheddar biscuits and country ham biscuits.

45. CHARLOTTE

Cowfish. The Cowfish, which now has a Raleigh location as well, is only genuine North Carolina in that it's delightfully eclectic and makes weird combinations work. It's a sushi burger bar. Yes, that's right; here you can grab an amazing burger or some divine sushi - or both. I don't even know what to recommend here; sometimes I actually don't choose this restaurant because I can't decide what I want and I can't possibly order six burgers and five sushi rolls. They've also created the burgushi, which is just the monstrosity it sounds like, except you have to keep an open mind because it isn't a monstrosity at all. I'm a fan of the Wooo-Shi Buffalooo-Shi Roll (although I am embarrassed to type that out and might write a letter to corporate about their item names), which is chipotle bison, fried green tomato, onions and feta in a sushi roll. I also love the Deliverance roll, a Southern style roll with pulled pork.

The Original Pancake House. Someone out there is going to lose their minds that out of all the amazing high-end restaurants and cultural classics in Charlotte, I listed a chain pancake place as a top three. But I did it and I'm not ashamed. Listen, it's the only place I've ever seen where you can get pumpkin pancakes year round, and the potato pancakes and dutch babies are no joke either. I'm not responsible if you venture into the lunch and dinner menu, and there's no need because you can get breakfast all day. There are other locations of this fine dining establishment in the United States, so you may be fortunate enough to be near one, but in North Carolina there are only two and they're both in blessed Charlotte. If you need a third restaurant suggestion in Charlotte and you're outraged about this one, I assure that Charlotte has some of the best dining in the state and TripAdvisor can't steer you wrong, but I stand by my insistence you try this place.

Dandelion Market. I've had everything on this menu because once I had two business trips to Charlotte in a month and on the first day I checked this place out. I had fried brie with plums as an appetizer and a main course of cherry glazed lamb lollipops, and I did not stop thinking about this restaurant until I went back...the next day. And the next and the next. They have my favorite shrimp and grits in the state and I have dreams about their pork belly.

Eat Like a Local

46. DURHAM

Rise. This goes out to everyone who screamed when I talked about biscuits and donuts and never mentioned Rise - I had a special place planned all along! I am pretty sure I have seen Jesus while eating the biscuits at this place. The bacon, egg, and cheese comes on a cheddar biscuit, which you might think means it doesn't need a cheese slice but you'd be wrong; in North Carolina we don't believe in cheese limitation. The fried green tomato biscuit can go on a buttermilk or a cheddar biscuit, and it's served with pimento cheese. My personal favorite is the country ham on a sweet potato biscuit. And yes, they have donuts too, and they're delicious. I'm a big fan of the maple bacon.

Bull City Burger and Brewery. There are approximately a billion great burger places in the RDU area, but Bull City is one of my favorites there and in all of North Carolina. They do an outstanding pimento cheese burger, but my favorite is the build your own burger, which starts at an affordable price but I can easily rack up to triple with all the add-ons. They also serve pickle chips, a baked sweet potato and sweet potato fries, and homemade ice cream that I can never finish but almost always beg someone to share with me so I can get a taste.

Saltbox Seafood Joint. The Saltbox is a walk-up with an atmosphere and menu inspired by ye olde fish camps, and it might sound humble but you'd be wrong if you think that. The owner is a trained chef and was inspired while on culinary travel in Singapore. It's so popular the owner produced a cookbook, and thankfully it includes his honey hushpuppies, which I've driven over an hour for. This is another place with a menu that changes daily but every Saturday you can count on my favorite, crab grits.

47. GREENSBORO & WINSTON-SALEM

Lucky 32 Southern Kitchen. This place, one of my favorites in all of North Carolina, has a location in Cary outside of Raleigh too, but the Greensboro site is the original. Almost everything on the menu seems to come with grit cakes and has at least a dash of Texas Pete, vinegar, or bourbon, like all proper dishes should. They also understand that a good shellfish, okra, and pimento cheese go with almost anything. They have the good sense to put Pot Liquor and Pickin' Cake right on the menu, the first of which I've never seen on a menu anywhere and the second of which most higher end establishments would be too snobbish to do. It's an amazing orange cake with pineapple in the frosting, obviously not North Carolina native ingredients but a native dessert and

Eat Like a Local

served at any proper pig pickin'. Other than the fact that it's actually called Pickin' Cake and we refuse to pronounce g's where they can be implied, I'm not sure why this masterpiece is mostly ignored in many finer establishments, but it shouldn't be, and Lucky 32 knows it.

Scrambled Southern Diner. Some of the plates at this diner seem like they took everything North Carolina and threw it into one dish. The concept works too; I could not possibly choose a favorite off the breakfast menu; just take ten people with you, order everything, and have everyone take a tiny bite of each. My favorite non-breakfast item is the PLT, in which bacon is replaced by pork and you won't be surprised by now to hear that it is topped with pimento cheese. They also have the good sense to plate fried green tomatoes not just with (of course) pimento cheese but with Neese's country sausage.

Milner's American Southern Cuisine. This place can be described in the same way as Scrambled, taking everything we call home and throwing it together, except at Scrambled you think "Why did I never think of that?" and at Milner's you think "What insane person thought of that and how fast can you get it to my table?" Have you ever thought of combining Moravian cookies, salmon, and sweet potato flapjacks? What about fried green tomatoes served as a "short stack", grilled chicken livers with Texas Pete mayonnaise, country ham and fried green tomato benedict, or pork with jalapeno and peach chutney and green tomato chow chow? They do all of that and they're geniuses.

48. RALEIGH

Relish Craft Kitchen and Bourbon Bar. My favorite thing about this place is that it's somehow between the greasy spoon mom & pop country kitchens and high-end places that serve up Southern food with a price tag that defies the thrift from which these dishes were borne. There's nothing on their menu that you haven't tried or thought of before and it's everything you want to eat. The grilled cheese with pimento cheese and fried green tomato isn't Carolina enough to be called the Carolinian; of course that honor was saved for the grilled cheese with pulled pork and slaw. They know what to do with burgers; of course they have a Carolina style but there's one with pimento cheese and fried green tomato too, and my favorite is one I've never seen elsewhere - homemade North Carolina peanut butter and bacon, a combination I'd never have tried at home and would have missed out on if I'd never tried there.

State Farmers Market Restaurant. The State Farmers Market in North Carolina is one of my favorite places in the whole world. In other countries, there are large commercial markets with product and chaos the likes

Eat Like a Local

of which most North Americans don't really see in our home cities. The first time I stepped into one though, I felt just like I'd entered my old stomping grounds. The North Carolina version is a relic going back to at least World War I and probably before, and it is packed over acres. There are three restaurants there managed by the state but to me the highlight of the entire compound is the one simply called State Farmers Market Restaurant. It's the most unpretentious place I've mentioned in this volume, serves mostly breakfast, and I like to get there somewhere close to its open time at 6:00 AM and fuel up before I spend my morning buying all the North Carolina-grown produce and craftwork I can fit into my vehicle. There's no menu item that is going to knock you off your feet but anything you try is pure North Carolina and makes the homegrown patrons feel like they're right back at their roots.

The Angus Barn. This place is so authentically ingrained in the culture of mid-Carolina that it's probably cliche, but that's also why it has to be included here. It's a steakhouse, and there are only a few items that sound like something you'd never heard of elsewhere, but I promise they're some of the best steaks you'll ever try. I'm a filet mignon person, pretentious though that may sound, but Angus Barn has one particular dish that isn't just a filet mignon like every steakhouse. The espresso rubbed filet is just that, over blue cheese mashed potatoes and with a red wine and chili reduction. Guess what? I can add pimento cheese and shrimp to that, and I can get a sweet potato on the side and blackberry cobbler for dessert, and that's after the barbecued ribs they had the good taste to offer in small enough portions they could put it on the appetizer menu. Don't scoff at me that everyone goes to the Angus Barn - of course they do.

49. WILMINGTON

I grew up in Wilmington and it's where I go back to when I'm in between travels; there is no way to list every place that deserves a mention here. Wilmington is a culinary mecca in North Carolina especially known for its seafood, but here I've chosen a few favorite places.

Pinpoint. What I love about Pinpoint is that it's not just authentically North Carolina but it's authentically Wilmington. I'm not aware of any other restaurants frankly anywhere in the world that get that real. The menu is what we grew up on right there in the city, back when it wasn't so big and didn't have all the international flair it does now. They list their suppliers right on the menu, so as if I could make anything taste as good as the prizes that come from their kitchen, I can go buy produce and seafood directly from the source. Almost every time I have

Eat Like a Local

eaten here I've gotten so excited about the appetizers that I fill up and have to get my main course repackaged to take home and eat later. You can order local raw oysters one-by-one, served with lemon blackberry granita and cocktail sauce, a hummus made with butterbeans and green tomatoes, and candied pecans aren't just a snack here from a can but actually on the menu. The menu changes regularly but when they have pork chops or catfish, I can't get there fast enough. The selections on their vegetable plate change regularly but it's always the veggies I pushed aside on the plate growing up but here are presented in ways I would never have thought of and can't get enough of.

Love, Lydia. This charming little place is a bakery owned by the former pastry chef at Pinpoint. She also happens to be the fiance of a former owner in Pinpoint who dabbles in her kitchen as well (and was nominated for a James Beard award this year, super-cool in a city that often gets overlooked for our culinary talent).

One observation I have made about mid-sized cities like Wilmington is that small bakeries and cafes often lack the originality of those in big cities and the authenticity of those in small towns, and Wilmington isn't an exception to that problem - but Love, Lydia is. It's a bakery, so the offerings change daily, but you can't go wrong with her coffee, biscuits and

85

brownies, and I live for her soups, even though I am the first person to tell someone "I hate soup."

Manna. Doors here opened in about 2010, roughly when I moved away from Wilmington, and sometimes in between visits I mourn not being close enough to eat here. The first time I went I was on a date. I frankly didn't like him, and I couldn't decide between literally everything on the menu, so I called everyone I could think of to join an impromptu dinner party so I could sample it all and not talk to him. The occasion was his first time in the place as well, and I never saw him again except for twice when he was eating at Manna again, both times with the same woman who I assume is now a long-term partner, so I'm glad that worked out for him.

The menu changes often but you can always count on pork and seafood here, and they make a sourdough loaf that really is, well, manna. I mean they actually call it that, because they know it too. I still go to Manna in a large group so I can have a little bit of everything.

Casey's Buffet. This nondescript building is another place that people who are only looking for the Mannas and Pinpoints of the world are going to be confused about, but when I go home if Manna is manna then Casey's is Mecca. I can't eat there very often because frankly, I'm afraid I will die, but if I eat quinoa and a few kale salads for a couple of days

Eat Like a Local

before to convince myself I pre-gamed my body, I go all in.

It's an all you can eat buffet of every monstrous food a true North Carolinian has ever loved, and if you go on Thursdays at lunch they do Brunswick stew (that it's not daily is the only terrible, terrible thing about this place). I am usually incapacitated after eating here so if I go on a Thursday, I'm not working that afternoon. I'm not sure North Carolina invented the buffet (Is there an inventor of buffets? Or is that just something God did?), but we made it epic because we're also home to Golden Corral restaurants.

But I think the owner of Casey's Buffet must have been to a Golden Corral once, said "Honey, bless your heart" and went home and not just one but probably three-upped it. I don't know if Casey's has never been franchised because it would cause a national health crisis and the CDC forbade it, or if everyone who ever thought about approaching the owner about it couldn't follow through because of the food coma that happens after.

50. TWO BONUS RESTAURANTS IN THE MIDDLE OF NOWHERE BUT TOO GOOD TO LEAVE OUT

The Gamekeeper in Boone is my favorite restaurant in the world, and if I've already said that five times, cancel the others, because this is the one. Somehow I never knew about this place when I went to college at Appalachian State University in Boone (probably because I survived on burritos and beer), and having missed out on it back then genuinely makes me sad. I have built entire weekends out of road trips across the state and up the mountain because I want to eat at The Gamekeeper, even though I will pretend it's to visit family and friends, or go to some silly insignificant event like Homecoming or a wedding.

They have plenty of food for vegans and vegetarians, and herbivores love this place, which blows my mind because the reason it's called The Gamekeeper is that the main dishes are not just beef and trout but bison, elk, emu, and duck. As far as I can recall I have never seen chicken or turkey on the menu; that would just be far too common. Honestly it amazes me that I've never seen PETA picketing outside.

I always get the okra salad (which, don't be surprised, has country ham and pimento cheese) and duck with honey mashed sweet potatoes and a blackberry ginger glaze, although if it's not available for some reason I

Eat Like a Local

am perfectly fine with almost anything else on the menu.

Chef & the Farmer. This now famous location is in Kinston, where I have had to stop saying "there's nothing in Kinston" because I'm pretty sure the existence of this restaurant drew the attention to put it the place on the culinary map. Now the town boasts Mother Earth Brewing (and some other really great breweries, but they're my favorite), Boiler Room Oyster Bar (which is owned by Vivian Howard, mastermind of Chef & the Farmer), the Whiskey Pig Craft Butchery, and Middle Ground Coffeehouse, which is great anyway but is the only coffee shop in Kinston.

All of these places opened after Howard gained national attention for the tired little town with her first restaurant, which she opened with the intention of helping belly-up tobacco farms convert to food crops. As the granddaughter of a tobacco farmer who had a rough time when the crop lost its value, that's a movement I can get behind with pure joy in my heart. Howard hosted A Chef's Life all about eastern North Carolina cooking traditions on PBS for five years, and she started the show because she feared the food traditions were starting to be lost and needed to be documented.

Howard also owns Benny's Big Time Pizzeria in Wilmington. "Benny" is her husband Ben Knight, also a chef who works alongside Howard.

CONCLUSION

You can't just eat good food. You've got to talk about it too. And you've got to talk about it to somebody who understands that kind of food. - Kurt Vonnegut, writer

North Carolinians know good food, and they know some pretty strange food. But while most people think of food as nourishment, we view it as community too. There is nothing better than coming together over a delicious meal - whether it's one of our many food festivals or a family event, the daily meal table, or a gathering with one of our social groups, we rarely eat alone. If you really want to eat like a local while you're in the Great North State, invite along your family and your friends, catch up, and laugh or cry - some spiritual sustenance over the physical sustenance before you.

OTHER RESOURCES

You didn't think I could limit this to fifty tips, did you?

Our State Magazine https://www.ourstate.com/
One of the best travel magazines published, and it's all about North Carolina. This publication celebrates North Carolina travel, food, and culture. Check it out for endless restaurant and adventure suggestions.

Food & Drink Trails in NC
https://www.visitnc.com/story/XnG7/dig-in-food-drink-trails-in-north-carolina
I mentioned the Sonker Trail because it's an authentic North Carolina dessert with little recognition, but it's not the only culinary adventure in the state. This list offers up nine others and they're superb.

North Carolina Food Tour Suggestions
https://www.tripadvisor.com/Attractions-g28954-Activities-c42-t204-North_Carolina.html

North Carolina Restaurant Suggestions
https://www.tripadvisor.com/Restaurants-g28954-North_Carolina.html

NC Craft Brewery Map
https://www.ncbeer.org/nc_craft_brewery_map.php

NC Winery Map
https://www.ncwine.org/wineries

North Carolina Food Taste Test
https://www.youtube.com/watch?v=8nqulZwskoU

The North Carolina Barbecue Trail
https://www.youtube.com/watch?v=II_fsUDY_5s

READ OTHER BOOKS BY CZYK PUBLISHING

Greater Than a Tourist- St. Croix US Birgin Islands USA: 50 Travel Tips from a Local by Tracy Birdsall

Greater Than a Tourist- Toulouse France: 50 Travel Tips from a Local by Alix Barnaud

Children's Book: *Charlie the Cavalier Travels the World* by Lisa Rusczyk

Eat Like a Local

Follow *Eat Like a Local* on Amazon.

Made in the USA
Monee, IL
03 May 2023